A Raven's Heart

A Raven Cave Anthology

Poetry Collection

I0142464

AP Publishing
Los Angeles, California
December 2017

An AP Publishing Publication

Compiled by Angel Wings and Kasey Hill
Edited and Formatted by Kasey Hill
Cover Art by Kasey Hill

Copyright © 2017 Elias Raven Productions
All Rights Reserved

ISBN: 1-945987-35-9

ISBN-13: 978-1-945987-35-9

Ordering Information:
Quantity sales and special discounts are available on quantity purchases by U.S. and International trade bookstores and wholesalers. For details, contact the publisher at the address above.

Printed in the United States of America

For Veterans and for the Children of St. Judes

Foreword

Hello Everyone,

What you hold in your hand is something very precious. Anything given as a gift to help others is always something special. The wonderful men and women that compose my fan group are some of the most caring and loving people I know. When I first approached them about writing a cave anthology for charity, without hesitation, they volunteered for the project. You, the readers, get to take in and absorb this wonderful gift of poetry and prose that is laid before you like a fine offering on a banquet table. For many of the members of The Raven Cave that asked to be a part of this anthology, this will be the first time that they have ever been published.

I am proud of the many that are part of this. I love to watch seasoned veterans work alongside those that are just dipping their toes into the literary waters and then all come together for the greater good.

I love to watch people encourage and build each other up. For some, this was a scary proposition. I watched more then a few walk through their own fears and cross over the chasm of insecurity and doubt to bring forth poems that, until this release, have never seen the light of day.

Courage was the watchword along with a lot of cajoling as we raced together toward the finish line. I want to personally thank all of you for helping me and my partner, Sharon Johnson, accomplish another dream... This will be the first anthology published under AP Publishing.

Thank you to all of you for making that a reality.

A very special thank you goes out to Kasey Hill from "Azoth Khem Publishing," whom is also a very dear friend, for volunteering and doing the cover design, layout, formatting, and most importantly, double checking the editing along with helping with all the legalize for this release.

Another big thank you goes out to Angel Wings for gathering all the poems and working alongside of Kasey Hill compiling the anthology and helping with all the minutiae that goes into getting a book ready.

Thank you all for this very special gift and for taking this journey with us. I know the charities will be grateful for the donations and anything done that changes people's lives is always something to strive for on a daily basis. In these troubled times, we are grateful to publish this small beacon of light and hope that you enjoy sitting by the fire and reading as much as we enjoyed creating it for you.

Happy Holidays Everyone...

Elias Raven

"No one is useless in this world who lighten the burden of another."

—Charles Dickens

"The meaning of life is to find your gift. The *purpose of life* is to give it away."

—Pablo Picasso

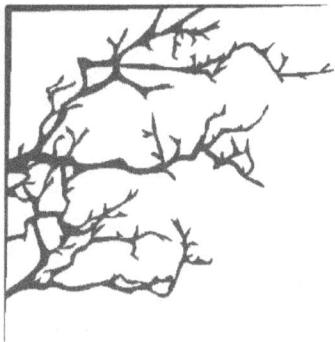

Smoke me Out
Kasey Hill

Every room in my mansion
Is filled with beautiful things
To cover the scars on the walls
Hiding away my broken wings
Let me take you to my special place
The room I lay in at night to sleep
Don't look at the walls in here
I haven't had a chance to bury anything
Or paint the walls white or black
The memories in this room
Keep coming back
Feeling me with a sense of doom
The dread that washes over me
Makes me feel lost inside
Like I am running a marathon
But my legs won't move from being tired
I crawl across the finish line
Waiting for the applause
But in my desperate state

I was abandoned by them all
I swear its like I'm always late
When I have no place to go
My inner alarm clock is chiming
But there's nothing to silence or show
It's empty in there
A house of broken dreams
It's why I built this mansion
So I can try to breathe
But someone is setting fire to the place
It keeps spreading room to room
I know they're trying to smoke me out
But I am not a fool
I see them watching me through my window
Knocking trying to bring me to the door
Last time I acknowledged them
I said I wasn't answering anymore
The fire is burning through the house
Slowly burning my beautiful things
What they fail to realize when they're gone
My memories are free forever to haunt me
The walls are fireproof
Trapping the fire around me
Since I can't escape this room
I will just smile as the fire surrounds me
Consuming me in the heated wall
Without me here
All those memories
Will finally be gone
© 2017

Time
Kimberly Cortez

The clock strikes Midnight
This is when you step out
Of the past and into the present
Looking forward to the future
Remembering the ones lost
Appreciating the ones found
Honoring those who are loved
Protecting the unprotected
Life is short to have regrets
Make opportunities for yourself
Take chances in life and love
you will be surprised for sure.
This is a new beginning for many
Embrace the changes that will occur
Always learn from past mistakes
and let nothing or no one stop
You from being the best of you
© 2016

I See You
Julie Beckford

I have heard you say
Time after time
I'm right here are they blind?
No they see your aura your light
But from time to time
We forget to acknowledge the ones
That mean the most
We take for granted
That they will always be there
We know that you have our back
When we need it most
With a helping hand or an ear.
So don't think for a minute
That you are invisible
Because that's far from the truth
I see you every where I look
When I see someone else
Giving a helping hand

Or an uplifting word
I see you.
You can't hide.
I see you
Right by my side
© 2017

Me

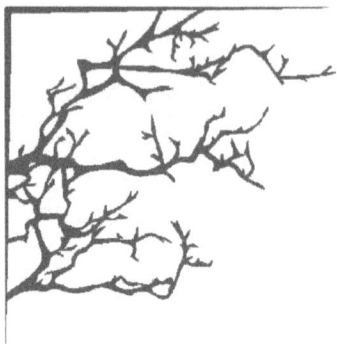

Lucy Roderick

Composing
Trying to put some words together
To hopefully make some sense
Is like trying to build alife
While sitting on a fence
So many words to choose to write
My mind goes numb
With writer's fright
And sometimes the words
Get stuck in my head
Even at night when alone in my bed
Life is often lived
In spiraling emotions
Seeking that one who gifts
Everlasting devotion
Creative juices flow
Sometimes fast, sometimes slow
Always working
From a past of dark vision
That simply won't let go
Helpless… is sometimes how I feel

'Cause I don't have nerves of steel
© 2017

Symphony of Our Souls
Crystal Kennedy Stoyanoff

He sat silently in his chair with a tender yet
hungry look upon his face
I crossed the room to him and his bow as he
closed me in his warm embrace

He molded me to him like a cello, his instrument
of choice
The bow felt like feathers across my hot skin
When his fingers brushed my spine my skin
tingled and rejoiced
At last it was time for our symphony to begin

It started off sweet and soft
It mimicked how we met
HIs gift was definitely Heaven sent

It wasn't long before his bow took flight
With our bodies entwined

The passion and storminess of the movement was
just right
He continued to play me until our hearts were
aligned

Our shared gasps and moans were our only
metronome
When the music was finished I collapsed in his
arms and knew I was home

When I could I again looked upon his radiant face
As his muse I knew beside him forever was my
place

No words could express our rhythmic tryst
The fire and adour of the music left me concise

This was OUR Symphony
Our Symphony of OUR Soul
© 2017

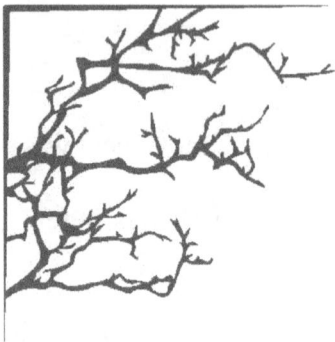

Rest
Roux Cantrell

Rest now your tired head
And heavy heart
Beneath a canopy of stars

Smile for me
I will settle your mind
With a kiss

You'll dream of me,
I of you
And we will never
Be alone in the dark

When the moon steps aside
For the morning sun
I will turn to you

Snuggling deeper
In your loving embrace
© 2017

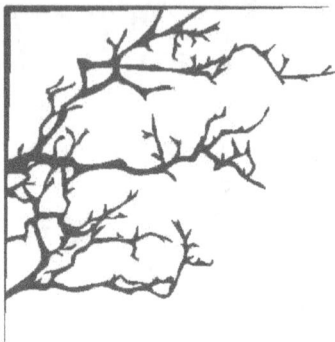

Blue Eyed Boy
Eunice Jáquez

Blue-eyed boy so sweet and kind
Happy and loving
The apple of his mother's eye
Playful younger brother
Protective big brother
Sweet blue eyed boy.
Happiness becomes sadness
Sadness fuels anger
Anger settles like a dark cloud
Unease, loss of trust, and fear reign
Blue-eyed boy takes the brunt
Shoulders the pain
Protecting his mom
Protecting his family
Wanting to ease their pain
Wishing the blood, bruises, and sadness
Would disappear
Still a playful younger brother
Always the protective older brother
Full of love for his mother
Who was spared a life of fear?

Blue-eyed man so strong
Trying to keep scars hidden
Fighting them as they attempt
To break through the surface
Attempt to haunt his dreams
Blue-eyed boy so loving
Always wanting to do what is right
Always giving others a voice.
© 2017

Weakness
Iris Magyar

Trying to always be strong
At times that's just wrong
Through your weakness you reach
For help and others may teach
A new way to see
For being happy
You give in to tight embrace
Leaves for flight no space
Slowly leaning on
Tightness easing - a bit gone
Not anymore so alone
Give it a chance
It might enhance
© 2017

Siren Song
Leah Negron

So enchanting and melodious
Drawing all men to her beauty captivating them
While her voice bewitched them leading their
ships
Aground to crash upon the rocks
So mesmerized where they that their
Deaths were swift
Leaving her to wait for another
Ship to sing her Siren's song.
© 2017

A Shattered Vase
Maggie Cotton

The pain I felt from loving you
Tears I've cried, you have no clue
I gave the key to my heart
All you did was shred it apart
You promised never to cause me harm
But you came and left like a storm
You broke me; I am now a shattered vase
You scattered my heart all over the place
Now my heart needs time to mend
So I will lock it up like it should have been
Till one day you will see
A new love come and rescue me
With gentle hands and eyes of fire
He'll make me burn with desire
With just one kiss I will see
How true love is meant to be.
© 2017

Deceit
Lynn Wolff

You were my 'everything'
My 'Knight in Shining Armor'
You were generous and kind
An undeniable charmer

You stole my heart
And had me believe
That I was your 'One and Only'
So how could you just leave?

You disappeared without warning
Without giving me a clue
And I discovered some time later
That I was someone you had to pursue

The lies, the deceit
It is now crystal clear
It was a bet between friends
"Make her yours for a year"

You were generous, smart
And acutely sincere
Was it all worth it?
Because your prize is still unclear

Now I am alone
With a broken heart
And finding it hard to continue
Since my world fell apart
© 2017

Chained
Girty Thompson

I kneel before you
A tempter of fate and seduction
But touch me you don't
As I beg on the altar of imperfection and need
A soul bound and twined Tethered to you
By chance
By accident
Neither one of us knowing where it would lead
Neither of us knowing where it ends
But I still sit at your feet
Prepared to stay
Prepared to go if wanted
My mind and heart conflicted with choice
Conflicted with envy
Envy of freedom
Envy of releasing these chains
But they do not clatter to the floor
And I don't want them to
I want to be bound to you

But I want to be claimed
Claim me you do not
But the chains tighten with each step away I take
Each fluid motion in any way but toward you
Sucks the air from my lungs
Makes my heart feel like it's dying
I am forever yours if wanted or not
You own what's left of me
And the only person
To ever hold my soul
© 2017

Both Sides
Teresa Crumpton

He is my dear brother
And yes I know
He's rough and tough
See though he can be sweet and kind
I love him so
But know that I see both sides
And even if you love him too
Don't see through his rugged side
It is there and it will stay
'til he's old and gray
So if this side is hard and cold
Love may go away
But please remember what I say:
I love him so, but I see both sides
I'm not the family that you see everyday
I'm the sister that sees his ways.
© 1998

THE ROSE
Vivetia Adams

Where everything was nothing
But dark and death around me,
I look for some sign of life anything
A bird
A tree
Anything that could make me feel alive
And not alone
And not as dead
As the landscape around me,
As I walked I spotted something pink
As I got closer I saw it was a rose
Blooming through all this death around it.
It showed it was a survivor
Just as strong and beautiful,
This one beautiful thing
Showed that life never ends
It just begins anew....
© 2017

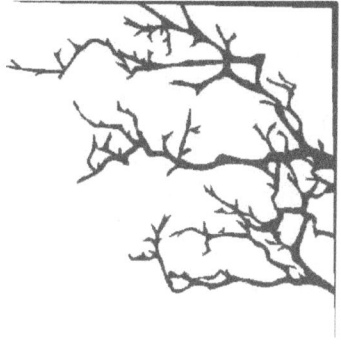

A Tango in the Moonlight
Laura Batton

You take my hand as the music begins,
Pull me closer
My heart skips a beat
I'm almost afraid
I will step on your feet.
You hold my chin
To look me in the eyes
And tell me try
You may be surprised
The rhythm is sexy
And sweet as we sway
To the music
And our bodies meet.
To feel your arms around me
Holding me tight
As we dance under
The soft moonlight
My pulse races

As you spin me around
I barely feel my feet
Touch the ground.
A night full of fun
And passion galore
I wonder what else
You have in store.
© 2017

Fall
Darcey Tilford

The fall season
has arrived
Trees changing into
Beautiful colorful leaves
Slowly falling down and
Spreading their magic spells
Preparing for winter's cold slumber.
© 2017

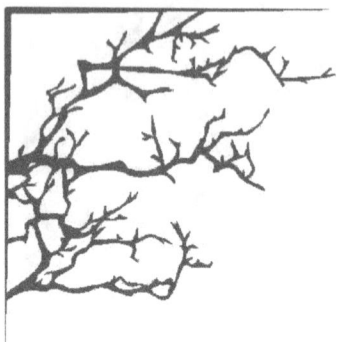

Idaho Sunrise
Lynn Stevenson

As the morning sun rises
Ready for a brand new day
Filled with hopes and dreams
Wishing they'll come true one day

The colors of its rays
Shining on the fence
The path leading to a happy home
It suddenly makes sense

Just A beautiful morning
Somewhere in Idaho
Two people reconnected
Letting their friendship grow
© 2017

Tragic
Athena Kelly

Scratching, clawing, always fighting back.
Trying to escape every attack.
It wasn't long,
as they were strong.
I was so weak.
I was afraid to speak.
Struggling for every breath I took.
Scared of every single look.
Never knowing what's in store.
Hiding behind my bedroom door.
Along came a loving man,
who kindly took my hand.
Pulling me from the depths of despair,
from the place where no one cared.
© 2017

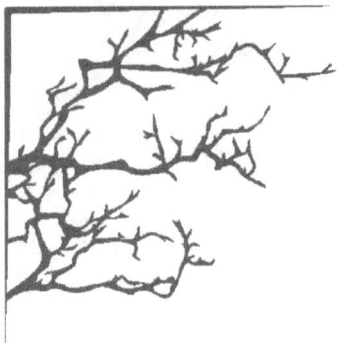

Only You
Carrie-Ann Hume

I don't know how to explain
the way that I feel,
but I know in my heart that it is
definitely real.

This whirlwind is scary
it happened so fast,
how do I show you
I want it to last?

We'll learn together
we'll continue to grow
one day at a time
no matter how slow.

There's so much we didn't
do in the time we had spent
but with a promise of forever
we'll do the things we're meant.
© 2017

Who am I?
Anna Pulla

What defines me
My looks
My accomplishment
My family

Am I less then others
No husband to call mine
Never carrying a child of my own
Always putting other first

Do my actions speak loud
My compassion
My patience
My love of life

I love my family
I love my friend
I love me
I am just me an no one else
© 2017

Mother's Prayer
Missy Harton

I didn't hear
His subtle cries
Oh God, the fear
Seen in his glossy eyes

How is it possible
A deviously speechless
Demonic beast
Seems completely unstoppable

I missed the signs
This failure all mine
Please allow him to find
The real man buried deep inside

To beat this addiction
Takes willpower and courage
Strength and support
There's no other prescription

With imperfections and flaws
Always be in his corner
Tending the wounds
From life's ugly claws

Be the gentle hand
To cushion the blow
For in a moment of weakness
His mind and spirit are no longer whole

Lord grant me the sight
For this mothers gone blind
I long to see the light
Return in my baby's eyes

Be his shield
His armor and guiding light
Prepare him for the vicious battles
That face him in this infinite fight
© 2016

Daughters
Sorrow
Sherry Morris

Why bother to have me
You let me down and drown in sorrow
I feel so hollow
Where is the caring when I needed it most
You are a ghost
Pinning away for dad which did not care about us
He shattered the trust
Left without a care
You blame me for his leaving
I understand your grieving
But would you feel the same
If you knew…
You are always hurling verbal abuse
For being shy quiet and introverted
You never once wanted to know why
I am the way I am
I know that you always wanted a son
What about a daughter
One who will not falter
One who is a fighter
One who knows she has a wealth of inner strength

So I am asking why can't you be proud of me
Well judging by your silence I must let it be
I have set myself free to be me!
© 2017

We Are
Sharon Johnson

We are...
The women of the cave

Some were...
Broken, scared and scarred...

But together...
Becoming fierce, determined
~And brave~

Where once...
We felt isolated, unsure and alone

No longer...
Do we feel voiceless
We now know there are...
~Choices~

No more...

Running here and there
Look around you'll find support...
~Everywhere~

So many...
Stepped out on a limb

Taking a big chance
Willing to share with others...
Our past hurt and circumstance

Supporting each other
Wives, daughters, friends and mothers

We are...
The women of the cave!!
© 2017

The Silence

Tracy Leroux

Silence sucks
What did I do
What happened
Is everything ok
Will I ever hear from you
Why do I feel I did something wrong
How can it hurt
Why do tears want to fall
Will I ever hear anything from you again
What if:
I hurt your feelings
I never hear from you again
I can't survive
I don't want too
Something is wrong
How:
Will I know if something happened
Can you mean this much
Can I get people to understand
Can friendship be this strong
When:

Did this happen
Will it disappear
It must be in my mind
A friendship that happened so quick, but means so
much.
Now all I hear is silence
Is it over
I will never know if something happens
No one to let me know
Do I just cherish the time we had
Do I keep messaging with hopes you answer
So much is said with silence
© 2017

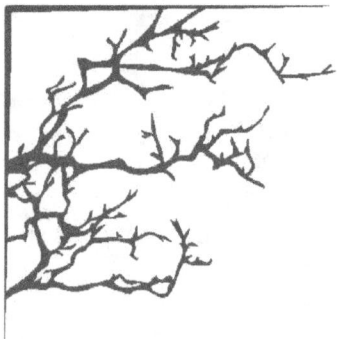

Haiku 1
Denise Jury

Wings of the raven
A harbinger of sunset
Blackness of midnight
© 2017

FRACTURED
D.M. Purnell

He stands there,
with silent stare.
See him quiver,
as he starts shaking.
Bleeding internally,
his heart is breaking.
Step you forward lend a hand,
can your soft touch mend a man.
His eyes glaze over,
back steps he takes.
Take more than your touch,
as he puts on the breaks.
More timid than that which is wild,
false bravado fragile as a child.
Silently you wonder,
if you could kill.
The one who did this,
with free will.
Don't give up,

the steps you take.
Will mend this man,
before he can break.
© 2017

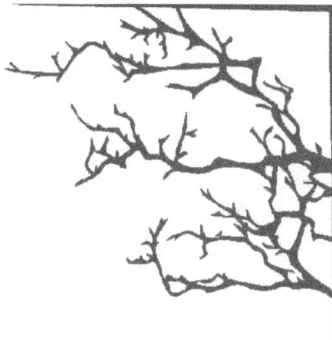

Kiss me in the Rain
Daphne Caldwell

Kiss me in the rain
Let me feel
The heat of your passion
As the raindrops
Caress my body
Let me see the beauty
Of your love
Touch my mind
Feel my heart
Reach my soul
Kiss me in the rain
© 2017

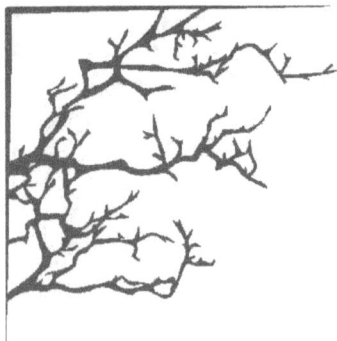

Vengeance
Angel Wings

The Sound is deafening
As I sit in silence
thoughts are threatening
My soul for violence

Anger is holding
My body hostage
Life is unfolding
My heart is in bondage

Blame assigned
Acceptance uneasy
Retribution denied
An existence left queasy

Justice to come
In the future I pray
For a reaper will run
Through the heart one day

A child of innocence
A soul betrayed
Is this a penance
At the feet to be laid?
© 2017

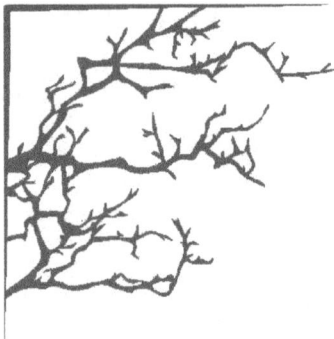

Barbed
Lea Winkleman

Your words cut so deep
A knife in me
Not once did I do
Anything to harm you
Turning blame unto me
Your way of feeling supreme
When will you take any claim
To what broke the chain?
Never were we meant to be
I settled for you
Thinking we could
Now the time to part has come
You push the barb in
Not once did I say hurtful things
I even took some blame
All alone I sit here thinking
How will I pull myself up again?
Then I look deep inside
Realize what I need to fly

No more barbs to my heart
The last one tore me apart
Time to undo this chain
Fly free and get home again
The support I need I have found
All around me I hear the sound
The wolf I know will keep me safe
Undo these barbs of hurt
Healing time has come to me
Time to be free
From the barbs of hate
No more bleeding
My heart will do
Time to heal me again
© 2016

Simmering Regret
Elias Raven

I hated the call
the lingering
as of yets...

A parents worst regret...

Was I good enough...

Did I teach them
the right way...

I listen to your
stammering excuse...

At times...

I don't know
if it is a ruse...

A blind alley
to thrown off
my keen eyes...

I don't mean to pry...

Your business...

Your life...

No matter how
much strife
and turmoil
you sow...

The garden
of discontent
now grows
like a weed...

The seeds spread
and blossom
throughout my soul...

More often then not...

Disbelief is my answer...

Incongruity gives
the tale a sense
of wonder...

Like a tornado
blundering
through our lives...

Rendering down
the essence
to get to the truth...

A sort of ruthless
blind man's bluff...

The huffing and puffing
to add effect...

Like talking
to a crazy uncle
rattling endlessly
about the end of days...

The perturbations
of the universe
strike a chord
of discordance

My soul screams
for some sort
of revelation...

A divine light
to show you

the way...

I will remain a voice
in your wilderness...

One of the uncool ones...

While your millennial
friends make excuses
for your lack of
common sense...
© 2017

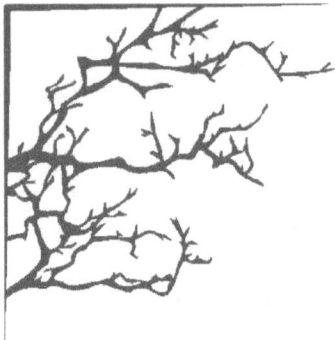

Trapped
Kasey Hill

I feel trapped
in this god-forsaken place
The fucking walls have been talking to me
Day after day
Telling me how it all ends
I can't breathe
as they swallow me whole
Inching their way closer to me
Squeezing out the ones I call friends
Soon there won't be anyone
Left in the end
After I push them all away
Every time I close my eyes
Fear ensues
Blacking out the daylight
I swear it makes it harder to breathe
Claustrophobia, paranoia
They slowly settle in my mind

I swear I used to be free
But the demons in my mind
Have been talking shit again
They tell me death is coming soon
God had no angels to send
Only demons are left to befriend
With just one more agenda to their plan
To drag me down to hell
A place I already live in
Man I need some help
But I won't reach out
This is my own hell
That I have to fight to get out
All on my own
© 2017

Why
Kimberly Cortez

You were larger than life
But through out the years
You have become so small
Just a shell of your old self
Why did this happen
You were once a social butterfly
But now afraid of your shadow
Loved being outside and free
Today locked away in darkness
Why did this happen
You are become the child
And I have become the parent
Our roles have reversed now
So many emotions being felt
Why did this happen
Give me the strength to handle
What needs to be done now
Give me the knowledge to know

What is the best for both of us
Why is this happening
© 2016

My Other Half
Julie Beckford

We met on a fluke
On Facebook two halves of a whole
Two connected souls
My go to girl that always has my back
It's funny they say
That couples who finish each other's sentences
Are soul mates
Well we aren't that kind of a couple
But are friends until the end of time and beyond.
My devil's advocate
For lot's of situations
When I doubt myself.
My partner in crime
Even though miles separate us
We talk about everything and nothing.
I would truly be lost without her
My angel, best friend to my devilish nature
we are the best parts of each other.
Can't have one without the other

It's just not right; to separate us would be a great
loss
Because we are halves of whole one connected
soul.
© 2017.

Who are they?
Lucy Roderick

Who are they
Who lie in wait
Or prowl the world
To control other's fate?

What is this they believe
And why are they taught
To damage innocents
At all costs?

And how can we stop them
Foil cruelty's plan
Of terror released
All over our lands?

We'll continue to walk
With heads held high
They'll not hold us down
No matter how they try
© 2017

Dad
Crystal Kennedy Stoyanoff

You were so scared the day I was born
You said your "hands were too big and I was so small"
In your arms I knew you'd NEVER let me fall

You overcame your fear and held me tight
You promised and you always did keep me safe at night

When I was 5 do you remember The Easy Bake cake?
It looked such a fright
Yet you told me how delicious it was, after you ate EVERY last bite

When I was 6 I went off to school
Despite your nerves you tried to remain calm and cool

From softball games to music I always saw you in
the crowd as you cheered
With you for my Dad I NEVER had any fears

You thought I didn't listen to you as you taught
lessons about life
I did...but it wasn't until I was grown that I
realized you were right

Now I have a child of my own
Remember when he was small you were once
again afraid to hold

God gave me the BEST when he gave me to you
This DAMN thing called cancer will take you
away from me way to soon

You're fighting this disease as hard as you can
I promise your grandson will know your life
lessons and become a Great man

I am Blessed to call you my Dad
I'll be there when the time comes to hold your big
hands

I'll remember every moment, love and lesson you
instilled
I Love You Daddy and I ALWAYS Will
© 2017

A Whisper
Roux Cantrell

I stand wishing for more time,
When we wonder why we let life
So often get in our way

That no more hugs will we share,
Not one more kiss will I feel

I hear her say

I am the warmth that soothes you
And the joy in your heart

The reason you take the path less traveled,
I am the curiosity around the bend

So know this

When a faint memory comes into view
When there is but a whisper left, know it's me

And

That I am with you
© 2015

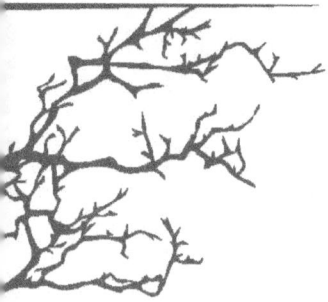

A Dream

Eunice Jáquez

Deep in sleep
She felt his arms around her
His lips bestowing soft kisses
All over her body
The ice in her heart
Melted at his touch
It soared with the freedom
His love gifted
She knew the significance
Of this dream
And wished for its reality
She looked for the clues
That told her he wanted her to stay
Searching his eyes carefully
Preparing herself for his answer
Already missing
The gentleness of his touch
The passion in his kisses
That toppled her shy demeanor
She hoped for this feeling

To last a lifetime
The standard they would
Live by...always.
© 2017

Light
Iris Magyar

Summer breeze
Feeling at ease
Warming beam
Soft stream
Light infusing
Soul soothing
Taking a break
Tension shake
Breathing free
Joyful glee
© 2017

Slipped Away
Roux Cantrell

I fight each day
Through emotions
That aren't mine

My eyes still bright
But, their getting tired

My soul that once soared
Pray its wings will mend

I fight each day
With a weary heart
That is mine

My body feels
Like a battered cage
With shaky hands
I reach for more

The empty light
That warms no more
A brilliant thought
Has slipped away
© 2016

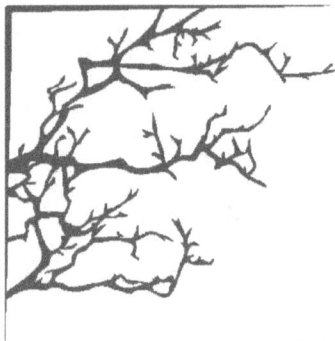

Unanswered Prayers

Leah Negron

She sat on the swing
With her head bowed low.
Crying tears for all
The sorrow in the world.
Unhappiness and misery
Is all she has known.
Depression setting in
Because of all the regrets she has felt.
Every day she tries to cover
The world with love and peace.
But to her dismay it's not enough
For one Angel to do.
The world is being torn apart
By hatred, discrimination,
Bigotry and so much more.
So many unanswered prayers.
She hears all of the sorrowful
Prayers of the believers
Praying for help.
She prays endlessly for
The sound of silence.

For the day she hears no prayers
Will be the day when
The world has become one.
No color, race, creed, or religion just
The human race.
© 2017

Love is Worth the Fight
Maggie Cotton

Love is not easy, nor is it perfect
It's hard and sometimes it hurts
But when you have to fight for it
You'll finally see Love's true worth
Temptations will always be there
It is the ultimate test
It takes strength and willpower
To stand strong, to never quit
So fight hard and give it your best
When their happiness is more important than your
own
You'll know Love was worth it all
So smile in spite your problems
Laugh through your pain
Fight hard for the one you love
Don't let your bleeding heart leave a stain
When the universe finds a way to keep you
together
You know your Love is real

So stand strong and believe
Love is worth the fight.
© 2017

A Chance Meeting
Lynn Wolff

It was a warm Saturday morning
And a lot was on my mind
I had decisions to make
And a whole life to leave behind
I was sick with worry
And my thoughts were elsewhere
I was nearing my destination
Not far from the Town Square

As I rehearsed my conversation
That was long overdue
I was not paying attention
And ran right into you
I knocked over your coffee
And sent your papers flying
I was extremely embarrassed
And I felt like crying

You reached for my hand

And looked into my eyes
And in that moment
You had me mesmerized
You began to reassured me
That everything was ok
And started cleaning up our mess
So we could be on our way

That simple act of kindness
Meant so much
You were a chance meeting
That I knew I couldn't give up
I took a deep breath
And pushed my troubles aside
For I knew there was no way
That this was goodbye
© 2017

When Does the End Come?
Girty Thompson

Walk with me you asked
Down the sands of imperfect love
Love that is forbidden
Sinful
Take my hand you asked
As we walked down this road
Not knowing a direction
Not knowing a plan
Just lost in one another
Leading one another through the dark
Awaiting the sun to show us our progress
But it fails to rise ceaselessly
The end of the path cannot be seen
The start of it long gone
I trust your guidance
I trust where you lead me
But please don't be silent in this envelope of black
torture
Tell me what plagues your mind

What plagues your heart?
Because I feel your hand losing grip
And alone in the dark I cannot walk
You have been my eyes at night all along
© 2017

This was Not the Way you Should Have Gone

Teresa Crumpton

Now was not the time to go
You helped your time
And for that you had to die
I wish you would have thought
But you didn't
You had to party and for that life is done.
I am angry with you, and I hope it passes
You finally got what you wanted;
I showed my feelings
You made me cry again
Although this time I can't stop
And you can't tell me you're sorry
You will always be in my heart
My friend, I hope you are in Heaven
So one day I can see you again.
© 1999

SHADES OF LOVE
Vivetia Adams

Our love has no color
It's nether black or white
Or that, which is in between,
It's an aura
It's a feeling that is stronger
Than anything you could imagine.
So you see the shades of love
Is many
And who you love
Is the greatest gift you could ever give...
© 2017

My Love
Laura Batton

My love
I know you are here with me.
I feel you
As you wrap me in your arms,
Your protective wings
And hold me close
Let me know I am not alone.
I have always felt safe, loved,
Treasured and adored
Even now as I am here
In this secret place with you
I know I will be always.
In life you were my King
And I your Queen
And not even death
Can separate our great love.
© 2017

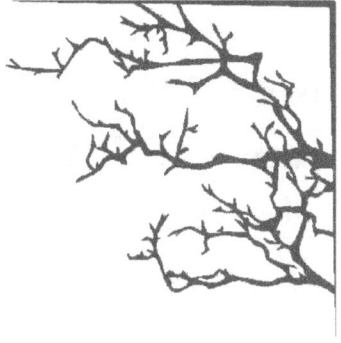

Dear Diary…
Darcey Tilford

A beautiful single rose unexpectedly laid on my
desk
My heart leapt with excitement
Wondering who this mysterious person could
be… someone I knew or someone new
A beautifully written note:
Your beautiful angelic face warmed my heart and
soul I want to keep you safe in my arms   and to
protect you with my life ~ Your Secret Admirer
It brought me a huge smile on my face
Oh the suspense was killing me
I desperately wanted to meet this mysterious man
I safely tucked the rose into my diary
With anticipation will he be able to warm my
heart and soul too?
© 2017

Shattered
Lynn Stevenson

Another rough night
A tear stained pillow
A broken heart
Without you by my side
Words cut like a knife
Leaving a big scar
I never imagined
You would cause so much pain
in my life
I'm feeling numb
And nowhere else to go
How on earth
Could you ever hurt me so
For better or for worse
Words to live by
I no longer feel the strength
For yet another try
© 2017

Our Love
Athena Kelly

Our love for each other is so strong,
I've always known it can't be wrong.
As I gaze out at the star filled night,
I know our future is just as bright.

Our love for each other is so pure,
Through all things we will endure.
As I gaze at our beautiful child,
I remember the days when we were wild.

Our love for each other is destiny,
As we were always meant to be.
As I gaze out at the cloudless sky,
I know we will be together, even after we die.

Our love for each other - so bold,
It only gets better as we grow old.
As I gaze back at our life,
I am oh, so proud, to be your wife.
© 2017

My Heart
Carrie-Ann Hume

You are the sun that
brightens my day
you are my missing piece.

I always knew that
something was wrong
but with you I feel complete.

Side by side
we'll walk this path
wherever it may lead.

Together holding hearts
and hands, like it was
always meant to be.
© 2017

I Won
Anna Pulla

This is me
No where to hide
I am real
My wrinkles and my scars

My pain
My bruises, my stitches
My aching bones
I know that was not love

Life has never been easy
I have had my highs
I have had my lows
But I would never change a thing

I am a survivor
I have beat you
I am no ones victims

I thank God for my strength
© 2017

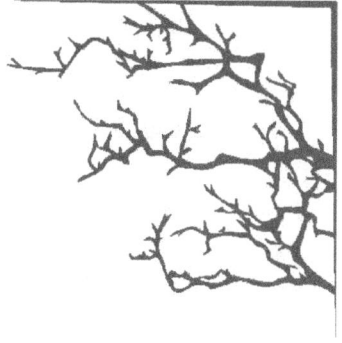

The Tolls of Depression
Missy Harton

You tell me you love me
You tell me you care
That look in your eyes, just isn't fair
Seeing a vacant cold empty stare

Your words hold no meaning
Their lack of effect has me pleading
Searching to renew
What first made me fall for you

I feel you slipping away
Don't know how to make you stay
As the demons inside
Slowly bury you alive

I need to be strong
Continue to carry on
Waiting while you seek
The inner strength to break free

There is no shame
For no ones to blame
Depression is a burden
Although I'm certain
In due time we'll find
Your lost sparkle and make you shine
© 2017

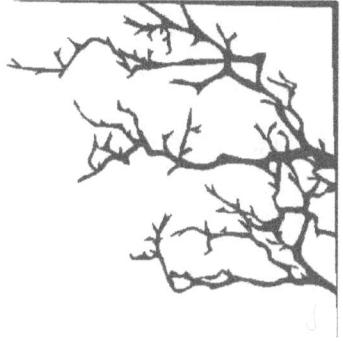

Musings of a Dark Mind
Sherry Morris

In death there is silence and bliss
So beautiful that I hear it calling to me
And wonder would I be missed
There is this emptiness that will not let me be
Will I ever be free
There is this light at the end of a tunnel
My mind feels like a funnel
Wide open then narrows
Would I be able to reach it with the help of a
sparrow
Only time will tell with this mental spell
Along came a tiny little sparrow
Chirping and flapping its wings encouraging me
to follow
Leading me out of the abysmal tunnel
Towards the beautiful bright light
Basking in the sun's full rays
This mental spell has broken
For I have spoken

Peace and enlightenment has filled my mind body
and soul
© 2017

I wasn't Wanted
Sharon Johnson

I wasn't wanted…
~As a child~

I can still feel the painful sting
~In my heart~

Memories sometimes haunted
My past taunted…
~Me~

A child's falling tears
But no one could hear…
So many… of my fears

Being left behind
Through all those painful years

Where were you?
And why weren't you…

My hero?

Things can't be changed
Never rearranged...
~From my past~

Life isn't a Hallmark moment
Parents aren't perfect

Some...
Even less so

But I've always thrived
Will always survive...
~Somehow~

You didn't break me...
Didn't make me
Into...
~Who I am~

I've become stronger
Outgrown
My perception

Of the lies to my recollection...
That you tried to teach
Tried to preach...
~To my heart~

Now as I look back

There's nothing that I lacked
Except…
The truth

I was born to be…
The woman people now see
The perfectly imperfect…
Uniquely special…
~Me~
© 2017

He Will Miss You
Tracy Leroux

Your little boy will miss you...
How could you not change for him...
How could you let him down...
At four he already knows you are a liar...
It breaks my heart to hear him say those words...
"Mommy, Where is daddy? Why did he lie
again?"...
I don't know what to say...
So I say "I don't know sweetie… Just remember
that he loves you"...
I give him a hug and kiss...
And then he is off to play...
You are going to miss everything...
His birthdays, his plays, his games...
I hope the drugs, the drinking...
The stealing and lying were worth it...
Because you are going to miss the most important
things...
Our son could have given you...

His hugs...
His Kisses...
Him saying I love you...
© 2017

Haiku 2
Denise Jury

Minutes change to years
Happens in front of our eyes
The passage of time
© 2017

QUEST
D.M. Purnell

Once a great wizard,
put forth such a test.
To look for the heart,
in the finding a quest.
Leaving on the trip,
were brothers three.
Warrior, Alchemist, and Wizard to be.
Behind them unknown,
was the last of their score.
The smallest but he,
would get there before.
Saving them all,
from a terrible fate.
By taming the dragon,
who protected the gate.
Shocked they all were,
their hearts stopped with fear.
At finding their baby brother here.
He told them to stop,

it was a silly quest.
To go out to look,
for what resides in your chest.
© 2017

Longed For
Daphne Caldwell

He comes each day and patiently waits
Seeking always seeking inner beauty
That he knows within
Never speaking silently waiting, knowing
That with diligence and perseverance
He will break her walls and
Crumble them to the ground
Then, ever so tenderly
He reaches
He touches
He whispers to her soul…
Ever so quietly she welcomes at last
A love she's always longed for
© 2017

A New Beginning
Angel Wings

A beautiful smile
A warm embrace
Innocence stolen
Without a trace

Struggle for acceptance
To never succeed
Beaten and battered
Even with a mothers plea

Pushed to the edge
No where to turn
Death would be better
For in hell I burn

A saving grace
A change of heart
A life is saved
Healing will start

A new day dawning
Life starting anew
Faith returning
With the morning dew
© 2017

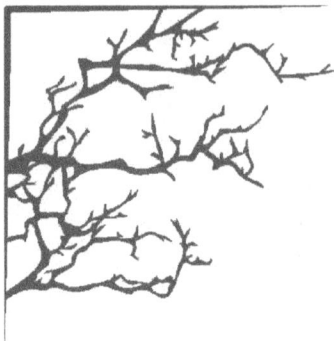

Hate Breeds Hate
Lea Winkleman

Hate breeds hate
Just as love breeds love
Respect of one another
Is what I'm thinking of
Too bad we have lost that
I am here to reteach all
Society as a whole has forgotten so much
We need a new lesson of old
I come from the past
History I've seen
So much repeating I see
The mistakes we've made
The loses were many
Death is next as we forget the need
Respect and forgiveness
That is what is needed
In these times of trouble
Remember the positive
I am the soldier to come show

Your mistakes now you reap and sow
For you teach others the badness I see
Hate breeds hate
When you should love thee
Never judge one another
Until you walk in each other shoes
You don't know the truth
Heed my words one and all
Love, forgive and respect
That is the call
© 2016

C'est la vie
Elias Raven

I hated to find you
so emotional...

The frailty was
etched on the familiar
lines and wrinkles
of your face...

Your voice cracked
when I entered...

The Good Morning
was strained...

Was that a tear
I saw creeping
down your cheek?

I saw the dog's collar

in your hands...

Turning it over,
rubbing the name...

I'm sorry...

Seemed to be inadequate...

Coming from my lips...

Now I was seeing
him on my lap
covered in mud...

"You big lummox
get down..."

Wasn't going to
be said anymore...

It was like the silence
wrapped around
the statement...

I keep hearing
"Which way did
he go George..."

Over and over
in my head...

Like an old
Warner Brothers
cartoon...

Your heart always
was in the right place...

He was your child
through and through...

The hardest part
is the guilt...

Asking if we did
the right thing...

They don't
have a choice...

They trust us
to care for them
and love them
unconditionally...

No one likes
to see an animal
suffer needlessly...

You were there
for him when

no one else
wanted him...

He'll be waiting
when it's your turn
to climb the stairs...

I know your spirit
will turn around
to those that are
gathered and start
singing...

That's life, that's
what all the people
say...

You always did
like Frank...

And you wouldn't
want it any other way...
© 2017

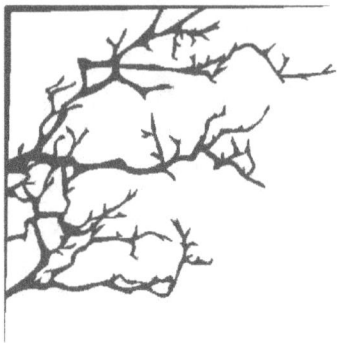

I Miss you Daddy
Kasey Hill

I remember daddy plopping me in his lap
Driving down the driveway in his brand new
Cadillac
I steered the car and he pressed the gas
And we both just laughed
As the wind blew through my hair
And held onto his hat
Fast-forward fourteen years to my senior prom
Daddy left the keys to his escalade
And gave instructions to my mom
Its her night to shine let her take it out
I remember all eyes were on me
As I pulled up in that Cadillac

How I miss you daddy
How I miss that smile
I miss your hugs I miss your laugh
I just want you back
Mama waited patiently

At heaven's gates
You two walked in hand in hand
A spectacle to be seen
But I still miss you daddy

As the years flew by my hero dad
Grew brittle and old in age
But his strength and determination
Was something that would never change
The one thing though that always
Remained the same
Was him behind the wheel
Steering that Cadillac Deville

You struggled in your final days
Never giving up once
You fought long and hard for us
Until your final breath
When they removed the breathing tube
And we stood by your side
I knew I had to you go
The man that hung the moon and stars
In my four year old mind
And now I don't know how to
Go On without you here
I wipe away that one stray tear
And whisper for you to hear

How I miss you daddy
How I miss that smile
I miss your hugs I miss your laugh

I just want you back
Mama waited patiently
At heaven's gates
A spectacle to be seen
Driving through St Peters Gate
In that pearly white Escalade
But I still miss you daddy
© 2017

Drift Away
Leah Negron

Some days life's journey
Becomes too much to handle
I just want to drift away
Float on a cloud
High in the sky
Carried away from all
The stress and woes
That weigh me down

I want a friend
Someone to ground me
In those lonely moments
Who understands what I've
Gone through in my,
Lifetime to make me want to
Just drift away

Maybe climb in
A boat and float away
With the tides
Listening to the water
Splash against the
Sides of the boat
Soothing a broken soul

Would you want
To float away or maybe
Drift away with me
One of these days
When life has gotten
Us down with
No way to come
Back around
From a world that's
Turned upside down
© 2017

No Second Chances
Lynn Wolff

You did not want me then…
~ You do not get me now ~
Time has passed
And you now realize
I was the one that got away…
But I did not move…
I did not run…
You were the coward
Who could not stay…
Time has passed
And my heart has healed…
Reinforced with a more
Protective shield…
One that you cannot…
And will not
Penetrate….
A shield
That can easily communicate…

~ There are no second chances ~
© 2017

I'm Endangered
Teresa Crumpton

My time is running out
But I am not the only one.

Many others are becoming endangered
Or extinct on this earth just like me,
Many animals that have lives worth living:
Beautiful animals like wolves, tigers, bears,
dolphins
and many more,
These creatures are graceful and brilliant.

We will be back with others one day.
They were hunters but became hunted by us.
My pack like many of theirs is dying.
Food spoilage, air heavy with pollutants,
Water dirty with toxins and no place to live
safely.

What can I do, no hope for us, not now, maybe
later?
So many are now dying.

We were many now we are few,
Are there others out there?

Yes, dear friend you are not alone.
There are many of us, endangered species,
As we call others and now ourselves.

We have caused most of the problems, We
Humans.
We created the pollution in the air, water and in
the ground.
We take away the land, from the animals
By cutting down trees and replacing it with waste.
We have caused this problem, along with many
other horrible acts.

We have started to clean up our actions,
But it takes time.
I hope it has come in time,
So we can bring harmony to the earth.

Hope is not lost; humanitarians will bring life
back,
To us and the other endangered animals. I'm
endangered

© 1999

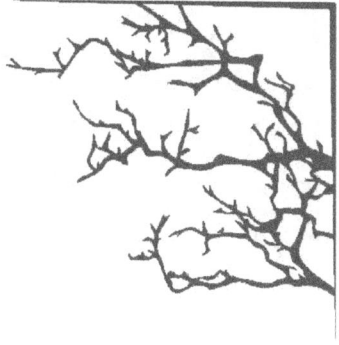

Touch
Laura Batton

When our eyes met I felt magic conspire
I felt such sudden desire
When you spoke the words "Hello beautiful" with
that smile so divine
I wondered is it possible you would be mine?
We talked a bit, walked down to the sea, and soon
thereafter
You kissed me softly
Something magical happened on that fateful day
I said to myself, this is surreal, yet come what
may
I believe in the heavens above, the angels sent my
one true love
That day I HAVE BEEN TOUCHED to the soul,
that day I became whole.
© 2017

Blinded
Lynn Stevenson

Blinded by your sweet words
Blinded by your love
Blinded by the way you made me feel
I could never get enough
Blinded by the way you cared
Blinded by the things you did
Blinded by the way you touched my soul
It almost made me scared
Blinded by your protection
but the benefit was yours
I never felt more stupid
It's time to close those doors
© 2017

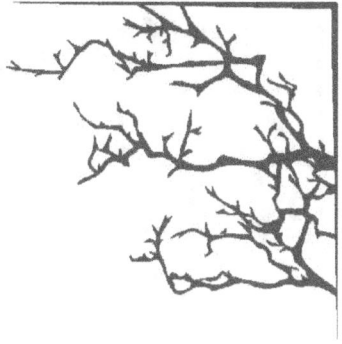

Why?
Athena Kelly

All the tears I cried
As I slowly died.
All the tears I didn't cry
As I hid them deep inside.

All the years I built a wall
As I struggled not to fall.
All the years I stood tall
As I tried not to drop the ball.

All the days I wouldn't let you in
As my heart and soul were steeped in sin.
All the days I couldn't win
As I wondered what could've been.
© 2017

Alive Again
Carrie-Ann Hume

I was barely surviving
going through the motions
a day-to-day life
without any emotion.

I gave up trying
after years of abuse
I started believing
that I was of no use.

Then something happened
right out of the blue
when I wasn't even looking
I somehow found you.

A light in my darkness
I could finally thrive
with you in my life
I feel so alive
© 2017

This is Me
Anna Pulla

I'm rough around the edges
I wear my heart on my sleeve
I'm fiercely loyal
This is me

I go with my gut feelings good or bad
I have my moments of shyness
I don't follow others
This is me

I am who I am baggage and all
My scars are hidden within
I am trying to leave them behind
This is me
© 2017

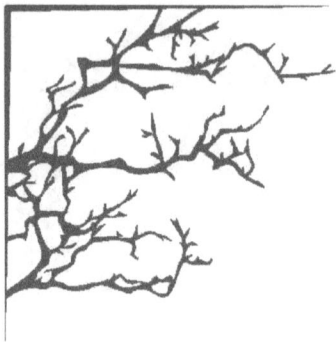

The Rose
Missy Harton

~Love~
Sacred beauty
Like the petals of a rose
Once pristine and pure
~Now~
Gracefully aging
New shades blossom
Revealing hidden strength
~Withered shell~
Vulnerable and fragile
~However~
Buried securely
In the heart of the rose
Precious images are etched
© 2017

Watcher
Sherry Morris

The guardian angel looked down upon the earth
Analyzing her worth
What is happening to this planet
The question in her mind echoing like a mantra
What is wrong with these humans
Do they not know what they are doing
To this beautiful planet they inhabit
For eons she has stood by and watched over them
Bearing witness to their destructive behavior
Now they seek a savior
From above the vast starts
Her voice booming like thunder across the lands
She calls out No More Wars
Tick Tock Tick Tock
Will they hear her in time
Before the trumpets chime
Procrastinate until its too late
What will become of their fate
The hourglass depleting fast

There is no half mast
© 2017

In A Dream
Tracy Leroux

I called you at the hospital...
You sounded tired and weak...
We didn't talk too long...
But you told me...
"I will call you when I get home"
Those words keep going through my mind
Will it be home, where you pick up the phone...
Or will it be home with your maker...
Will you come to me in a dream, and say...
"I'm home Tracy, and you know what, I feel no
pain"...
Will you talk to me in your voice like it was
before...
Before the cancer took it away...
Will you joke with me like you use too...
But now to tired to do...
I know you are in pain...
Scared to take anything to make it go away...
Afraid it will make you sleep...

Afraid to never awake...
I want you to know I love you, Papa...
I always will...
Just remember what you said...
"I will call you when I get home"
© 2005

Haiku 3
Denise Jury

Early morning mist
Rising from the mountain top
Beauty unfolding
© 2017

BANDITA
D.M. Purnell

Her emerald eyes pear at you,
from the mask of a bandit.
Her smile is,
sly and candid.
Her voice dares you,
to prove your manly.
Care to chance,
your future family.
Yet at her compelling figure,
dressed in satin and silk.
Skin soft sweet as milk.
You wonder if there is more,
to her simple slip.
Than the Jeweled sword,
in her grip.
Step toward her,
being crass.
She dumps you,
on your manly ass.
A whisper as she does pass,

want to try again.
© 2017

Pain
Angel Wings

Unworthy of love
Void of affection

No understanding
No direction

Ignored too long
Unable to recover

Forgiveness is sought
Understanding to discover

Relationships strained
Strangers meeting

Emotions refrained
Walls retreating

Keeping heartache at bay

Avoiding the pain...
Tears where I lay
© 2017

Ode to Marilyn
Lea Winkleman

She was a wonder
One of a kind
Always spoke her mind
Norma Jean was her name
Lost to soon to fate
All she wanted was love
All she wanted was to be herself
Time went by so fast
Wish we could whisper in her ear
What she means to many
When I hear Marilyn
I see beauty and grace
Never will we be the same
For a true icon graced our days
Now gone forever
Let the winds carry a message
Be happy to be you my dear
© 2016

Foundering
Elias Raven

Oh sweet slumber
how you elude me...

Must I see these
cursed visions?

Poor decisions...

My temple exudes
my distress...

Sheets soaked
in sweat...

I toss and turn
my dreams a tempest
of as of yets and regrets...

The memories
weigh heavy
upon my chest

If this be my fate man...

Then let it be quick!

My demise
is at hand...

The sand runs
through the glass...

Cold fingers pass
through my fevered
temple...

What was that?

My chest heaves
and shudders...

I gasp...

The chill runs
through my spine...

My emotions
are tossed about
like so much clutter...

Was that the whine
of a cat?

I am run aground...

Cursing my misfortune...

Pounding against the deck...

My bow broken
against the rocks...

Is this my penance?

O' Heavenly Father...

Come to me
in this dour hour
of remorse and pity...

The city of the damned
awaits one such as I...

My tears fall freely...

As I try vainly

To avoid my fate...

The stern beckons

for one more fateful ride...

I sit up straight
my voice splitting
the night...

As my emotions plunge
downward into the dark depths...
© 2017

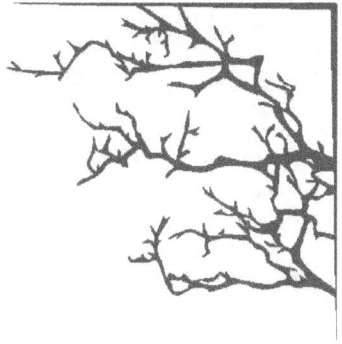

Behind This Mask
Anna Pulla

This mask is of such beauty
It's exuded sexiness
I close my eyes and put it on
I feel my mindset change

Behind this mask I'm free
I can be whoever I want
I can let myself go and enjoy
I can be who I'm meant to be

I am fierce
I am sensual
I let go of my inhibitions
I am the woman in the mask
© 2017

Puppeteer
Missy Harton

The evil magic puppeteer
Pulling strings
Weaving spells
Your life, I will steer

You will not complain
Nor disobey
I make all the decisions
If you wish for life to remain

Fulfill all demands
Swiftly and sure
To any commands
You'll respond with, Yes Sir

Hahaha...just wait
The game has begun
With you as my bait
We'll create wicked fun

For I am your
Evil magic puppeteer
Through my hands
Your life, I will steer
© 2017

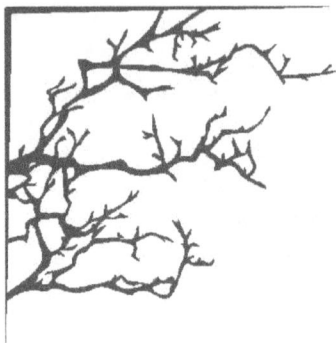

Haiku 4
Denise Jury

A single teardrop
Just hanging in the balance
For eternity
© 2017

Smile
Elias Raven

Some say
That every day
Should begin

With something nice
And easy

Even when you
Get queasy

And afraid
It's another day…

Everyone should have
Someone they can talk to

Someone to laugh with

Someone that makes

Them smile even when

Their head says not to

Some days are grey
And some days are way
Better than the last

But today is sunny
And the sky is blue

And I have a friend
I can talk to and laugh with

And that makes all
The difference

In my world…
© 2017

Poet Biographies

Kasey Hill

Kasey Hill has lived in Franklin County, VA for most of her adult life. Spending two years in journalism in high school, and a few articles published in the Franklin News Post, she built much of her young adult life around reading and writing. After being from the craft for a few years, she decided to get back into the creative writing flow. She has three novels published, (The Darkness in the Woods, Wastelands of Oz, and Firefly of Immortality) one novella (DOMbie: A Love Story) and many more stories circulating for anthologies as she pushes her passions forth into the writing community. Having published three poetry books (Dreams of a Broken Soul, Bittersweet Symphony, and Tiptoe through the Tulips) and a nonfiction book about Wicca, she began her path of becoming an established author. Now, along with her writing career and as former Owner and CEO of Jaded Books Publishing – an independent small press specializing in horror, she has merged her former company and the sister company, Azoth Khem Publishing. Now she is Vice President of Azoth Khem Publishing and acquisitions editor of horror, erotica, and poetry.

Follow Kasey Hill

- Facebook:

https://m.facebook.com/Kasey.Hill.Author/
- Twitter: twitter.com/kdt02201988
- Website: www.kaseyhillauthor.wordpress.com
- Blog: www.kaseyhillauthor.tumblr.com
- Pinterest: https://www.pinterest.com/kdt21/
- Goodreads: https://www.goodreads.com/author/show/11075849.Kasey_Hill
- Kasey Hill's Fan Group The Eclectic Quill: https://www.facebook.com/groups/1805999022997291/
- Group blog: https://www.facebook.com/the4horsemen18/
- Instagram: https://www.instagram.com/kaseyhillauthor/
- Editing page: https://www.facebook.com/NiteOwlPublishingServices/
- Google +: https://plus.google.com/112169881236347952709/posts
- Linkedin: https://www.linkedin.com/in/kaseyhill02201988
- Amazon: https://www.amazon.com/Kasey-Hill/e/B00O2WT210

Kimberly Cortez

Kimberly Cortez is a New York girl born in NYC and then grew up in upstate NY. https://youtu.be/XwOx_hWzsDM .She is the youngest of three daughters raised by a single mother. She was born with a speech impediment and struggled with finding her voice and as she grew older, she found it through poetry. She has had a few people that have mentored her along this journey. Elias Raven, Lea Winkelman, Don Abdul and Ethan Radcliff just to name a few. She started in this book community as just a follower and street team members for several amazing authors like Judith Anderson, JF Silver, KL Silvers, Don Abdul, Ethan Radcliff, Sharon Johnson and many others. She was given the chance of becoming a PA and assistant PA to Lea Winkelman, Riley Bryant, Pierce Smith, Amit Singh and Elias Raven. They have given her opportunities that she is grateful for. Kimberly became a published poet in 2017 when the author she was a PA for Lea Winkelman asked her to be part of her poetry anthology she was doing with fellow poets and friends. Dreams of an Empowered Soul was released and Kimberly was so honored to have been asked to be part of the amazing book. She can't wait to see what the future holds. Please follow her on her journey... Facebook: https://www.facebook.com/Kimberly-Dyan-Poet-1703868193212903/

Twitter:
https://twitter.com/dragonfly147
Instagram:
https://www.instagram.com/kimbers0171/?hl=en

Julie Beckford

Julie Beckford is a single mom of grown daughters and a serious dog lover. She has written a few poems not many more for enjoyment than anything else. She works full-time and pa part time for Sharon Johnson and Riley Bryant, and her Aussie author Ryan Baird. She also does video work for Elias Raven who's an amazing friend and teacher. She grew up in a very small town in Wisconsin and moved to a suburb of Chicago at the age of 16 to say it was culture shock is an understatement. Her nearest neighbors were cows. So her first trip to the city was awe inspiring to say the least. She has to say the indie book community is amazing. She met her BFF at an Ethan Radcliff TO and they have been inseparable ever since. Nola 2017 was amazing and if you get a chance go it was like a giant family reunion for days...

Lucy Roderick

Lucy Roderick is but a writer of words. She tries to express her deep feelings of love, heartache, and loss through her poetry "From My Blue Soul" and "My Bleeding Heart."

Crystal Kennedy Stoyanoff

Crystal Kennedy Stoyanoff is a mother to a wonderful sixteen-year-old son.

Most people don't know that she has always loved to write. Whether it's a poem or a story when a thought or emotion hits...she must write it down. If not, the ideas would beat her up inside of her head until she gave into them.

Crystal became fascinated by Edgar Allan Poe in junior high. His writing was so powerful and dark. It felt like she was being sucked into the madness that was inside his head.

Another favorite writer was O Henry. His works really made her think not just feel. He was very witty and his use of wordplay amused & amazed her.

Now, Crystal's taste in writing covers an extremely broad spectrum. Romance, erotic, horror, sci-fi and historical fiction now make up the majority of my reading style. The Indie writers have opened her eyes and awakened new reading interests within her.

Interacting with these writers has helped her start to open up and share some of her own works.

When Crystal is not reading or writing, she enjoys listening to music. She loves almost any type. She also played the saxophone & trombone and sang in honors choir.

Roux Cantrell

Roux Cantrell resides in Hammond, Louisiana, a cozy college town. Juggling a full-time job as a stylist and a growing family, Roux manages to throw some pretty outlandish Halloween parties where the guests have to adorn costumes to gain entrance. Potluck dinners and at least one motorcycle trip a year on her Harley are a must.

Her love of books started when she was very young and has never wavered. Years past, she didn't have time to write with a growing family; now, with the kids grown and out of the house, she writes her own adventures

Eunice Jáquez

Eunice Anne Jáquez is an amateur poet. She finds it easier to express herself in writing than in person. She has written poetry since she was in school and hopes to one day complete her first book, even if it's just for her eyes only.

Iris Magyar

Iris Magyar is a mom of three living with her family in Austria in Central Europe. She started her first tries at writing poetry as a teenager in German (her first language) and did that on and off. Later as an adult she came back to writing poetry and stories, but this time mainly in English. Encouraged by close friends she is now occasionally sharing tiny bits of her work.

Leah Negron

Leah Negron is a happily married woman with a love for animals and animal rescuing. She is a member of the Bayonne Elks 434 and Hudson County Animal League. In her spare time, she loves to read, write, and promote authors of all genres.

Having first appeared in Michael Gagain's book "The Lighter Side of Dark", she produced her first piece of published poetry leading her down the road to writing both poetry and short fiction.

Maggie Cotton

Maggie Cotton (Wildbutterfly MC) is originally from Louisiana but currently lives in Oklahoma. She has been with her wonderful husband for 22 years and they have a beautiful daughter that is 19 and getting ready to go off to NYU for college. They are very proud parents.

Maggie loves writing poetry, drawing and teaching sign language. She started writing poetry at a very young age. Around 11 years of age, she won both a poetry and drawing contest. Her poem was chosen out of everyone in my grade level and was sent in and published. Poetry runs in her family, both her mother Mona and sister Amy write poetry. Her husband and family have always encouraged her to keep writing and she is very thankful for them.

Lynn Wolff

Lynn Wolff is a busy mom of twins, who currently lives in the northeastern region of the US. She enjoys the warmer weather of the south and plans to move to Florida in the future. Lynn is an avid reader. She has always loved to read poetry, and just recently tried her hand at writing a few poems herself. Lynn is very excited for the opportunity to now share her work with all of you.

Girty Thompson

Girty Thompson was born and raised in the mountains of West Virginia. A writer of erotica, dark erotica, and dark poetry, she made her first debut in the anthology A Lovely Darkness through Jaded Books Publishing. A pure southern belle, she enjoys the outdoors and raising the animals on her family's farm in the southern part of the state. Soon to be published with Azoth Khem Publishing, she is raising the bar in poetry as the Dark Poet Queen. Look for her erotic releases Just Before Dawn and The Virgin Witch Diaries next year!

Teresa Crumpton

Teresa Crumpton, author of the Foster House Legacy Series, writes dark supernatural thrillers along with poetry, romance and short stories. She's been writing since she was a kid but never thought about being a writer until now. Teresa's first novel in the Legacy Series is a haunting ghost story with a little rumored family history within the pages.

Teresa obtained two degrees, Government with an Emphasis in Legal Studies, and English Lit, hoping to get into law school. In 2004 she married the man of her dreams. As they moved around the country her dreams changed. She once again went back to school, this time obtaining a Masters of Fine Arts in Creative Writing, and her writing became not only her passion, but also the fulfillment of a promise to her father before he passed.

Teresa Crumpton grew up in Cincinnati and Dallas/Ft. Worth, making her a hybrid Midwest and southern girl.

Vivetia Adams

Vivetia Adams was born in Philadelphia, Mississippi in the county of Neshoba. However, she was raised from a baby in Detroit, Michigan right across the river from Canada. She is the oldest of three kids that her mom and dad has. She likes to read, draw, listen to music and she doesn't consider herself as a writer. It's just something she likes to do for fun when the words hit her.

Laura Batton

Laura Batton lives in Oregon but is a California girl at heart where she is originally from. She is a romantic at heart and enjoys writing sweet and spicy poetic poems and stories. A dream come true for her.

Darcey Tilford

Darcey Tilford is an avid reader. She enjoys reading poems, quotes, and music lyrics. Before this anthology, Darcey had never written poetry until she joined the Raven Cave Fan Group. The group has inspired her to start writing poems. She is still learning as she writes. Besides poetry, she loves to do photography and drawing.

Lynn Stevenson

Lynn Stevenson started writing stories and poems when she was 15, but only recently she has had the confidence to share her poetry in a public place. Next to writing poetry, she has a voluntary job as Radio presenter and has been doing it since 2009.

Athena Kelly

Athena Kelly wrote a lot of poetry as a teen. She poured her anger and hurt into her writing. Sadly when all of her poetry was taken from her, she quit writing. Recently she received some encouragement from some friends to write again and to speak out about her past. The result was the poem "tragic". She is just beginning again and has only written 2 poems since her high school days. She has never been published before. She hopes to continue on her new path and to inspire others to never give up and speak out. Don't hide. She isn't anymore.

Carrie-Ann Hume

Carrie-Ann Hume is a mom of 2. Originally from Scotland, she is now living in Canada.

She has only recently started writing poetry again after 30 years. When she was a teen she fancied herself in a band. She and a couple friends used to write lyrics together. Family came along and it wasn't something she thought about doing.

This will be her first time publishing anything she has written.

Anna Pulla

Anna Pulla is pretty much a simple girl -
She is 50 years old. She works full time and is a caregiver for her mom.

Anna's passion is baking and cooking, which eventually she would love to have a successful blog and cookbooks. She wants to show people how simple it can be and be able to work with people in shelters, giving them tools to fend for themselves when they get out on their own.

Anna just started writing poetry. She loves sports, restoring old furniture, and when she gets a chance, spending time outside, hiking, meditating and practicing yoga.

Missy Harton

Missy Harton is an avid indie reader. She's made some unbreakable bonds with authors and fellow readers. From 9-5 she makes the "beef jerky" and spends her evenings socializing on Facebook, reading, or snuggling with her "Love Muffin!" She enjoys bowling, camping, and is an extreme NASCAR fan. She loves to spoil any and all little kids since hers have left the nest.

Sherry Morris
Sherry Morris was born in the Philippines but raised all over the U.S. Her dad was in the Military. She loves to read all types of books and listens to all types of music. She loves learning new and different things.

Sharon Johnson

Sharon Johnson has been writing since she was 6 years old. She had one dream to become an author. Year after year the book never came, until the summer of 2013 when a two to three page idea max kept growing. Soon after, it became clear her characters had much more to say and their story was far from over. That's how 'The Chat Room' was born. Eighteen months and a lifetime later, her dream finally became a reality in August 2015.

She's the co-author of 'Letters Away A Love Story' 'Letters Away A Love Story Prequel' 'Letters Away The Crossing' and Letters Away A Poetic Journey' written with Elias Raven author of 'Cain Sins of the Father' and the 'Painted Shadows' Poetry book

'Partners in Rhyme' is a poetry book co-authored with fellow poet, Ryan Baird author of Private Ryan Volume 1 She has several other projects releasing this year.

Sharon's other books include: 'Poetry of the Heart' a collection of twenty-five short stories. Each one ending with a perfect moment. "Life isn't perfect, but moments can be"
'The Eclectic Poet & Friends' It's an anthology featuring seven masterful poets and friends.
'Eclectic Poet My Voice'

'His Second Chance Love' the follow-up book to 'The Chat Room' Both are stand alone novels with no cliffhangers.

Tracy Leroux

Tracy Leroux was born and raised in a small town in Upstate NY where she still lives with her boyfriend and three children. She wrote her first poem on October 17, 1994, after receiving a phone call that her grandfather was very ill. From that point on, she used poetry as an outlet for what she was feeling. This is Tracy's first time publishing her work.

Davina Purnell
Davina Purnell lives in the desert southwest.
She lives with her husband who is sprucing up to
be her trophy husband, two dogs, one cat, her
youngest son, and his fiancé. She likes to hear
from her fans you can find her on Facebook and
her website.

Daphne Caldwell
Daphne Caldwell is the mother of 2 children, 4 grandchildren, and 2 cats. Originally from N.C. she now lives in a small town in Ohio and is a Proofreader for Indie Authors on line.

Lea Winkleman

Lea Winkleman is a busy mom of 2 boys. She lives in the sometimes cold & sometimes warm Midwest. Lea started writing as a teenager, but then stopped for a long time. She recently started back up again as a way to express her thoughts and feelings. As Lea began to share very slowly some of her work, she received more and more positive feedback. In the past two years she has written her debut poetry book Words from a Vulnerable Heart, which is being re-released. Lea on page 1has also written a second poetry book an anthology along with 11 of her most talented fellow poets and friends Dreams of an Empowered Soul. She is currently working on a third poetry book Asylum of the Broken co-written with Anakin Snider Ravenskraft. Lea is also currently writing an urban fantasy/sci-fi series with co-author Riley Bryant. Lea is very excited for the opportunity to now share her work with all of you.

Angel Wings

Angel Wings is from a small town in West Virginia. New to poetry, she uses pictures and experiences to pull her emotions out. She has two boys, and she currently works from home taking care of her special needs son.

Denise Jury

Denise Jury is a Canadian woman living on the west coast. She loves quilting, photography, and traveling; she is always looking for a new adventure. She observes, reads, and writes about her world through Haiku. She hopes to one day publisher her own book of Haiku along with her photographs.

Elias Raven

Elias Raven was born and raised in Los Angeles. He's an avid reader with a lifelong passion for writing. He's a storyteller, a poet and a talented musician with an amazing voice. Oh, and let's not forget an amazing cook!

As a young boy he spent many summers reading classics such as "The Adventures of Sherlock Holmes" and "The White Company" by Sir Arthur Conan Doyle. His creativity was constantly being pushed as he learned more and more about the world around him. His taste in literature spanned from classics to science fiction/fantasy. He expanded his taste devouring everything from William Blake to Milton, Dante, Baudelaire, Arthur Rimbaud, T.S. Elliot, Emily Dickinson, Robert Frost, Khalil Gibran, William Carlos Williams, Ezra Pound, Paul Verlaine, Walt Whitman, Alan Ginsburg, Jack Kerouac, William Burroughs, Carl Sandburg, Dylan Thomas, and Jim Morrison. These inspirations and his sheer love for reading had him take pen to paper around the age of 20.

Did I mention he's a Musician? ...You can often find him playing his guitars (both electric and acoustic) and keyboards and singing (4 octave ranges) in his home studio. He's a classically trained music aficionado -trained early on by Beethoven, Brahms, Mozart, Hayden, Liszt, as well as Big Band, Jazz and Rag Time. Spending time with his father at the Los Angeles Philharmonic; experiencing his first orchestra concert at the age of 9.

Elias the Gourmet Cook… Oh My! His Japanese mother and grandmother trained him very well in fine culinary skills both in cooking and food appreciation from all over the world such as Italian, Indian, Moroccan, Thai, Japanese, Chinese, Korean, Hawaiian, Pilipino, Greek, and Polish.

When Elias is not reading, writing, composing music or cooking…he can be found listening to music, playing games, hanging out with his kids. He enjoys going to concerts, going on culinary adventures, sightseeing, spending the day at the beach or in the mountains…just doing something adventurous!

Follow Elias Raven

- **Twitter: https://twitter.com/EliasRaven1**
- **Tumblr: http://eliasraven.tumblr.com/**
- **Instagram: http://instagram.com/eliasraven1**
- **Soundcloud: https://soundcloud.com/elias-raven/**
- **Website: www.eliasraven.com**

- Author Facebook Page: https://www.facebook.com/eliasravenauthor
- Facebook Music & Video Production Page: https://www.facebook.com/pages/Eias-Raven-Music-Video-Production/308963965959568?fref=ts
- YouTube: https://www.youtube.com/channel/UCuOQbFXDiSzgRk4sAYf0PNA
- Goodreads: https://www.goodreads.com/user/show/35827344-elias-raven
- Barnes and Noble: http://tinyur.com/qxo8ta8
- Smashwords: https://www.smashwords.com/profile/view/EliasRaven
- Amazon Author Central: https://www.amazon.com/Elias-Raven/e/B0160IV0A4/

Index of Poets

Index of Poems

www.ingramcontent.com/pod-product-compliance
Lightning Source LLC
LaVergne TN
LVHW051405080426
835508LV00022B/2979